CELEBRATING THE FAMILY NAME OF KUMAR

Celebrating the Family Name of Kumar

Walter the Educator

Silent King Books
a WhichHead Entertainment Imprint

Copyright © 2024 by Walter the Educator

All rights reserved. No part of this book may be reproduced in any manner whatsoever without written permission except in the case of brief quotations embodied in critical articles and reviews.

First Printing, 2024

Disclaimer

This book is a literary work; the story is not about specific persons, locations, situations, and/or circumstances unless mentioned in a historical context. Any resemblance to real persons, locations, situations, and/or circumstances is coincidental. This book is for entertainment and informational purposes only. The author and publisher offer this information without warranties expressed or implied. No matter the grounds, neither the author nor the publisher will be accountable for any losses, injuries, or other damages caused by the reader's use of this book. The use of this book acknowledges an understanding and acceptance of this disclaimer.

Celebrating the Family Name of Kumar is a memory book that belongs to the Celebrating Family Name Book Series by Walter the Educator. Collect them all and more books at WaltertheEducator.com

USE THE EXTRA SPACE TO DOCUMENT YOUR FAMILY MEMORIES THROUGHOUT THE YEARS

KUMAR

In lands where sun and shadow meet,

The name of Kumar strides complete.

A banner high, a steady flame,

A legacy bound to a noble name.

From verdant plains to mountain peaks,

The Kumar name in history speaks.

Of honor earned and courage shown,

A family strong, a name well-known.

Through ancient scripts and tales retold,

The Kumars' spirit shines like gold.

Their wisdom deep, their vision clear,

A guiding light through every year.

From scholars' pens to builders' hands,

The Kumars shape and guard the lands.

With dreams that stretch to skies above,

They plant their seeds of hope and love.

Through trials faced, they rise anew,

The Kumar name remains steadfast, true.

In every heart, their story grows,

A symbol of strength wherever it goes.

In bustling streets and quiet halls,

The Kumar legacy proudly calls.

A name of pride, of roots profound,

A harmony in every sound.

Their lives reflect the brightest star,

The endless brilliance of Kumar.

Through every era, bold and free,

They chart the course of destiny.

With every hand that sows the field,

The Kumar name its blessings yields.

Through work and care, they pave the way,

Building tomorrow, day by day.

A family bound by love's embrace,

Their unity time cannot erase.

Through countless seasons, near and far,

They carry forth the name Kumar.

So raise the song, let voices sing,

Of Kumar's strength, their hearts they bring.

A legacy vast, a future bright,

Forever shining, a guiding light.

ABOUT THE CREATOR

Walter the Educator is one of the pseudonyms for Walter Anderson. Formally educated in Chemistry, Business, and Education, he is an educator, an author, a diverse entrepreneur, and he is the son of a disabled war veteran. "Walter the Educator" shares his time between educating and creating. He holds interests and owns several creative projects that entertain, enlighten, enhance, and educate, hoping to inspire and motivate you. Follow, find new works, and stay up to date with Walter the Educator™

at WaltertheEducator.com

www.ingramcontent.com/pod-product-compliance
Lightning Source LLC
LaVergne TN
LVHW012051070526
838201LV00082B/3913